591.5 Colby, C.B.

Wildlife In Our
National Parks

DISCARD

WILDLIFE IN OUR NATIONAL PARKS
Birds, Reptiles and Mammals

by C. B. COLBY

Coward, McCann & Geoghegan
New York

Contents

National Park Wildlife	3
Wild Turkey	4
Ptarmigan	5
Hawaiian Goose	6
Roadrunner	7
Waterfowl	8
Salamander and Alligator	9
Diamondback Rattler and Gila Monster	10
Pocket Mouse and Kangaroo Rat	11
Pika	12
Jack Rabbit	13
Golden-mantled Ground Squirrel	14
Kaibab Squirrel	15
Prairie Dog	16
Hoary Marmot	17
Long-tailed Weasel	18
Badger	19
Striped Skunk	20
Marten	21
Wolverine	22
Porcupine	23
Muskrat	24
Beaver	25
Opossum	26
Raccoon	27
Coatimundi	28
Ringtail	29
Kit Fox	30
Red Fox	31
Wolf	32
Coyote	33
Bobcat	34
Mountain Lion	35
Black Bear	36
Grizzly Bear	37
Collared Peccary	38
Pronghorn Antelope	39
Mountain Goat	40
Mountain Sheep	41
Black-tailed Deer and White-tailed Deer	42
Mule Deer	44
Caribou	45
Elk	46
Moose	47
Bison	48

© 1965 C. B. Colby   All rights reserved.   Manufactured in the United States of America
Library of Congress Catalog Card Number: 65-20513

U. S. Fish & Wildlife Service: 13, 14, 19, 20, 21, 24, 27, 30, 34, 39, 43, 47 top; Colorado Game & Fish Dept.: Title page, 35; Union Pacific Railroad: 15, 46; Maine Fish & Game Dept.: 45 right. All others including full color cover transparency courtesy National Park Service, Department of the Interior.

Photographers: George D. Andrews, Leo K. Couch, R. C. Zink, E. P. Haddon, Roland H. Wauer, Donald Curry, W. P. Taylor, Joseph S. Dixon, V. B. Scheffer, Robert Flint, W. H. Marshall, Mrs. John Fabian, Abbie Rowe, W. A. Parter, C. H Henry, O. J. Murie, John C. Raftery, Robert M. Linn, L. J. Goldman, Don Domenick, Granville B. Liles, Bill Cross, J. Malcom Greamy.

Seventh Impression
SBN: GB 698-30410-1

National Park Wildlife

One of America's greatest assets is her wildlife. Since the days of the Pilgrims most species of wildlife have remained pretty much in evidence, if not in their original range, at least in some part of the country. Some tragic exceptions, due to man's thoughtlessness and changes of natural habitat, are the passenger pigeon, the bison, and the Florida kite. (There are several others in danger.)

The passenger pigeon is extinct, the bison barely missed a similar fate and the Florida kite, a hawk-like bird which lives exclusively on a certain snail, is facing extinction due to lack of this particular type of food.

On the other hand, several species are actually more abundant than when the Pilgrims landed. The Virginia, or white-tailed, deer has greatly increased its numbers, and the coyote, in spite of poison, traps and guns, has extended its range from the western plains east as far as New England.

One of the most significant and beneficial steps in the conservation of our wildlife was the establishment of our great chain of National Parks, administered by the National Park Service of the Department of the Interior.

Within the boundaries of these vast parks, which enclose over 20,000,000 acres of wild and beautiful country, no wildlife can be molested or killed. Control and balance of the species is left to nature and she usually does a superb job if left alone. The Park Service Rangers merely give nature a helping hand from time to time and see to it that she is not interfered with by outsiders.

One of the aims of the Park Service is to keep the population of species native to the park in healthy balance with the food available, and as far as possible, to keep exotic or unnatural species out of the area. For example, in some parks feral (domestic animals reverted to a wild state) pigs, goats, sheep, burros, and horses have entered an area in considerable numbers and are in direct competition for the food required by native species. These "foreigners" are removed as efficiently as possible, by trapping or other means, in an attempt to keep the area as natural as possible as far as species goes.

On the other hand, if certain species should be in an area but are no longer found there, they are frequently imported from other areas where there is an abundance to restore the original wildlife catalog of residents.

In all park areas there is transient wildlife passing through, which has always been normal. Unless these animals are unnatural to the area and linger, or present a really serious problem, they are free to travel through the park and go on about their business.

Occasionally the population of a certain species, particularly browsing or grazing animals (elk, deer, sheep, bison, etc.), increases to a point where the range or food supply will no longer sustain the herd in top condition. In that case the surplus animals endangering the health of the rest are removed by trapping and transferred to another area where food is plentiful, or harvested by Park personnel and the meat given to institutions.

This is far better than permitting the herd to starve itself to death or enter a period of semistarvation. Such a condition, if permitted to continue, would result in weakened and stunted animals and an increase in disease. It might take several generations before a semistarved species could be restored to original and normal vigor.

Removal of old, sickly, injured or diseased members of a herd to reduce its numbers will bring it back into balance with the food supply, before the healthy members begin to suffer. This is humane conservation at its best.

A visit to our National Parks will give you a chance to see many animals and birds native to the area, and often under particularly ideal conditions. Many of the animals can be seen along the park roads or from them, or at special feeding areas where they come in numbers to find food. Almost all of the species you will see on the following pages, with perhaps such exceptions as the wolf, mountain lion, and bobcat, can be observed, often at surprisingly close range.

I would like to acknowledge with sincere thanks the many in the National Park Service who have helped me with these photographs, many of which are remarkable. In particular I must give my warmest appreciation to Francis X. Kelly, Press Officer, who spent much time and effort to see that I had the best possible help and material. Without his enthusiastic assistance, suggestions, and cooperation, this book would have been impossible.

— C. B. COLBY

Wild Turkey

Although this handsome wild turkey gobbler is rare in the wild state today, he was once found from Maine to Florida. In fact, just stubborn arguments by those who wanted the bald eagle as our National Emblem prevented the wild turkey from becoming our national symbol instead of the eagle. The wild turkey shown here was photographed in the Wichita Mountains Wildlife Refuge, in Oklahoma. Many states are raising these noble birds for release in the wilds so that eventually they will once more be part of our natural wildlife. These birds stand over 3 feet tall, are 4 feet long and have a wingspread of 5 feet. They weigh up to 20 pounds. The hens are smaller and weigh half as much as the gobblers. They are elusive and shy but unlike the fat domestic turkey are powerful fliers. Wild turkeys are found in several of our National Parks.

Ptarmigan

There are several species of ptarmigan and all are important to the wildlife of the arctic and the high country south of the arctic. The white-tailed ptarmigan are found in Rocky Mountain National Park and in Mount Rainier National Park as well as some others. They are the smallest of the species and one of the rarer mountain birds. They average about 12 to 13 inches long and change color with the seasons. In summer they are mottled white and brown, making them very difficult to see even when close. In winter their color gradually turns until they are almost solid white as shown in the photo. They lay as many as fifteen (usual number about seven) eggs for their nest in June. Their nest is in a shallow depression in the ground lined with soft grasses and bits of moss. These handsome birds eat leaves, buds, insects, shoots and flowers, and usually stay above timberline even in winter. Although the ptarmigan is a fast and strong flier, it usually relies on its camouflage for protection from an enemy, often permitting very close approach before thundering away like a partridge or grouse.

Hawaiian Goose

The Nene or Hawaiian goose, shown here photographed in the Paliku section of Haleakala Crater, was at one time one of the rarest birds of all. In 1951 there were only about 30 of these big, strikingly black-and-white geese left in the world. Bred in Hawaii, England, and a few other spots these birds are staging an amazing comeback, to where there are about 400 of them in existence. Several of these are in the Haleakala National Park in Hawaii. Mongooses have killed some of them in spite of protective measures but it is hoped that the flock will increase to a point where the extinction of these rare geese is no longer a probability as it has been. Note the leg bands on the two geese in the foreground. These birds are about the size of the Canadian geese or "honkers" we see flying overhead in long "V's" in fall and spring.

Roadrunner

Protected wildlife soon learn that they have nothing to fear from man, and as a result they are often seen along the highways which pass through our National Parks. The author has met bear, elk, antelope, badger, bison and many more species along our fine park highways and from them seen many more, including many species of birdlife. One of the most interesting birds you are likely to see along our park roads is the odd-looking roadrunner, a member of the cuckoo family. This long slender chap is almost 2 feet long and seems longer as he races along the side of the road ahead of your vehicle. When he runs, his head and tail may be almost in a straight line as he skims along. He seldom flies unless really frightened, for he runs very swiftly indeed. He lives on lizards, insects and snakes which his great speed enables him to pursue and catch with ease. His color is brown and white and he has a white patch behind the eye. He has a crest on his head, a long strong beak and sturdy legs. This particular bird was photographed in Big Bend National Park, Texas.

Waterfowl

It does not take any species of wildlife long to discover sanctuaries where they are not molested, where the food supply is abundant and where nesting conditions are good. Almost all of our National Parks offer some species of wildlife, mammal or bird, all of these ideal conditions, with the result that visitors can often see several species of wildlife living together as in the fine photo above taken in the Everglades National Park in Florida. Here are wood ibis, American egrets, little blue heron, and coot, all feeding together in a calm slough in the everglades. At one time the snowy egret was at the point of extinction due to use of its fine plumes on women's hats. But thanks to the Audubon Society and many conservationists and their efforts, it was saved, just as we are now battling to save the great whooping crane from extinction. This tall bird, which is over 5 feet long with a 7-foot wingspan, was once with us in great numbers but by 1941 there were only 17 known to be alive. Now, thanks to great care and protection, there are almost 50, but it will be many years before they are really safe again. At many of our National Parks, guided tours are planned to show visitors many species of wildlife. When you visit our Parks be sure to take these tours.

Salamander and Alligator

Our National Parks, in which all wildlife and vegetation are completely protected, are sanctuaries for many kinds of wildlife. As a result species such as salamanders and alligators can easily be seen in their natural habitat. There are dozens of species of salamanders, amphibious creatures which spend much of their life in or near water. The largest of these harmless and interesting amphibians is the Pacific Giant shown above at top. These animals reach a length of 1 foot and are found in moist areas under rocks, near streams. They are smooth skinned and shiny with the back a mottled black and yellow. The eyes appear to bulge and have thick lids. They are found in our Muir Woods National Monument, in California. The alligators shown below in the Everglades National Park, Florida, grow to be over ten feet long and prefer fresh water, where they eat fish, turtles, eggs, birds, crayfish, crabs, and other aquatic creatures. There are also a few American crocodiles, smaller, thinner, and much more agile than the alligators, to be found in remote Florida park areas. These prefer salt water to fresh but dine on similar food. Both of these latter species lay eggs which are hatched by the sun.

Diamondback Rattler and Gila Monster

Typical of the poisonous reptiles in our National Parks are the eastern diamondback rattler found in the Everglades National Park, Florida, and the Gila monster, found in some of our desert and western Parks. This species of rattlesnake grows to be nearly nine feet long and is the biggest rattler of the several species found in our Parks. Some species are nervous, aggressive and may or may not warn by rattling before striking. All species live on rabbits, gophers, rats, mice and other small mammals. Their young are born alive and as many as a dozen may be born at a time. The Gila monster, our biggest and heaviest lizard and the only poisonous one, reaches 2 feet in length. Unlike a snake which injects its venom through hollow fangs, the Gila's poison is worked into the wound by chewing while he holds onto his victim. Most of a Gila's short curved teeth have two grooves, and the venom, expelled from glands at the base of the lower teeth, runs along these grooves into the wound. Gilas are usually slow moving but can twist their heads and bite swiftly, so do not touch them. They feed on mice, eggs and other lizards. They lay six to a dozen eggs. Both rattlers and lizards usually hunt after dark and live under rocks and in empty burrows. Do not put your hands in such places as one of them may be there waiting.

Pocket Mouse and Kangaroo Rat

There are almost countless species and subspecies of rats and mice in our Parks, so here are but two representative species. Top photo shows a little pocket mouse and lower photo shows a kangaroo rat. This little mouse is about 6 inches long including the tail. It lives in a burrow and closes the hole from the inside during the day, coming out at night to feed on seeds and plant matter. It can go for months without a real drink of water, getting moisture from the seeds and other things it eats. The kangaroo rat has short front legs and long hind legs, moving about in long fast leaps on hind legs only. Both animals vary in color, the lighter ones living in the desert. Both have several litters a year. The kangaroo rat has a large head and face, marked with two dark bands which extend from each eye back across its cheeks. Pocket mice have fur-lined cheek pouches for carrying food and are poor jumpers. Both of these rodents are found in Death Valley, and throughout the Southwest.

Pika

Up in Rocky Mountain National Park you can find plenty of these little chaps, known as pika, coney, rock rabbit, etc. Pika is the official name, and they are members of the same family as the hares and rabbits. They do not have any tail and like some other relatives in this family they whistle when excited. They live in small rock crevices and store lots of dried plant material in piles near their dens for winter food. The pika is about 8 inches long and weighs about six and a half ounces. It has several litters of young a year and the new arrivals weigh only about a third of an ounce. Pikas eat a great deal of grass and store even more — some of which may be eaten by sheep when food is hard to find and they can dig out a pika's store of grass. Pikas are brownish-gray in color and almost perfectly match the rocks in which they live.

Jack Rabbit

Although called "rabbits," these big long-eared rodents are really western hares. Hares' young are born with fur coats and their eyes open, in contrast to baby rabbits which are born naked and with eyes shut tight. Jack rabbits can jump as far as twenty feet and as high as 5 or 6 feet when pursued. They weigh up to 10 pounds and may be as much as 2 feet long. Sometimes the huge ears are a third of the body length. Jack rabbits live on almost any kind of vegetation and drink little water, getting what they need from the vegetation. They are a main part of the diet of coyotes, which often have trouble catching them because these hares can run at a speed of forty miles an hour. Once while horseback riding in Arizona the author had one of these speedy chaps jump clear over his horse in its haste to escape a pursuer. The Jack rabbit lives in thickets and does not burrow. In areas where they are plentiful there may be as many as 75 per square mile. There are several species of these long-eared Park residents and all are found in our West and Midwest.

Golden-mantled Ground Squirrel

Everyone is familiar with squirrels. There are so many kinds of squirrels — red squirrels, gray squirrels, chipmunks, and familiar western species — it would take a whole book to list them all, but here is a really handsome member of the clan from Mount Rainier National Park. The golden-mantled ground squirrel is a native of our western pine forests and found in areas where it can dig burrows for shelter and for raising its young. It also uses these burrows for hibernation in winter. This squirrel is about 10 inches long and is golden orange from its head back to its shoulders, including its front legs. The rest of the body is grayish and the white stripe down its sides is edged in black. It feeds on seeds, especially those of the pine, and also enjoys fruit. The tail (hidden here) is about half its length and is covered with short hair like the familiar chipmunk, which it resembles. It is frisky and friendly, often seen around campgrounds and cabins, looking for a handout.

Kaibab Squirrel

One of the most unusual of all squirrels, the white-tailed and tufted-eared Kaibab, is found in a very limited area on the north side of the Grand Canyon. This big squirrel measures up to almost 2 feet in length, and the tufted ears and white tail make it appear even larger. These squirrels have one or two litters of young a year and there may be three or four in a litter. Kaibabs live in areas where yellow and other pines provide them with plenty of seeds to live on, and also where they can find good places to build their nests. Their nests are pretty large affairs, composed of leaves, twigs, bark, grass, and needles, placed on a tree branch. In the winter these squirrels are not very active but actual hibernation is doubtful. The long ear tufts vary with the season but seem to be longest in winter when the rest of the coat is thicker. These squirrels resemble the Abert squirrel, common in Colorado. Except for the striking all-white tail, the Kaibab is dark in color — brownish-black on back and sides with black underparts. The author has a mounted freak gray squirrel which is also all black with a pure white tail tip. Perhaps he wanted to be taken for a Kaibab relative.

Prairie Dog

These small western neighbors are related to the ground squirrels but are larger and more social. They run to about 14 to 17 inches in length and live in prairie-dog towns sometimes numbering hundreds of these animals. They live in burrows and can be spotted sitting up by the entrance or close to it. At the slightest sign of danger — hawk, coyote or camera-fan tourist — they give a shrill whistle and vanish down the hole. The author has photographed many of them near Devils Tower, in Wyoming, where they are used to tourists and will sit for their picture if you do a little silent stalking to get close. There are two varieties, the black-tailed, most common, and shown here, and the white-tailed, less common. Both varieties have four to six young in the spring and live almost exclusively on grass and other green vegetation. The white-tailed clan prefers higher country and mountains and does not make conspicuous mounds of dirt by its burrow. There used to be millions of these sociable little animals but ranching, farming and general perils of civilization have reduced their number greatly.

Hoary Marmot

The hoary (meaning grayish-white in color) marmot is a western relative of the eastern woodchuck and resembles him. These marmots live in rocky areas, often high in the mountains, where they can build their dens under rocks to escape enemies. Their enemies include coyotes, foxes, wolves and bobcats as well as an occasional mountain lion. Their call is a shrill whistle given in time of danger. Besides the hoary marmot there is also a yellow-bellied marmot which is less gray and has a yellowish underside, hence the name. Both types live on plants almost exclusively and do not require much water. They have a litter once a year and the small-fry number from two to five. The young often spend their first winter in the same den with their mother and usually leave their parents when the next litter arrives the following year. The adult marmot may weigh as much as 15 pounds and reach 30 inches in length.

Long-tailed Weasel

There are many kinds of weasels and all are very difficult to photograph. This photo shows a long-tailed weasel in winter outfit, all white with a black tail tip. His winter coat is known as ermine, the traditional fur worn by royalty for hundreds of years. These weasels average about 16 inches in length while some other species are smaller. These animals are what one thinks of when the word "weasel" is mentioned, for they are lightning fast, vicious fighters and destroy millions of mice every season. They also kill birds, poultry, and rabbits and eat many eggs and insects. They hiss and scream when fighting and one species or another is found in almost every part of the country. They live in dens, usually underground, and have one litter a year of from three to ten offspring born in almost any month. The long-tailed weasel may weigh up to 15 ounces.

Badger

Those of you who live in or have visited the western part of our great land may have seen this big member of the weasel family, shuffling along looking for food and grumbling and wheezing as though he had asthma, or was short of breath. He weighs about 24 pounds and is about 30 inches long, if a big one, although the average is somewhat smaller. He is a fierce fighter and will fight bravely and with skill against great odds, often beating a coyote or bobcat who thought he would be easy prey. The badger lives on ground squirrels, snakes, birds and eggs. He can swim and climb well, if need be, and can burrow out of sight almost before you can dismount from a horse. He is grizzly-gray and black with a striking white stripe from nose to shoulder and white facial markings. They have up to five young in a litter born in early spring. They live about thirteen years in captivity and keep their dens very clean and neat. They also have a vile spray like a skunk which they can use as a weapon.

Striped Skunk

Most every part of the country has skunks, especially this striped one, so it is no wonder he is found in our National Parks. There are several other types of skunks — the spotted skunk, the hog-nosed skunk and the hooded skunk. All are basically the same, and black and white in color. They all belong to the weasel family as does the fellow on the opposite page. Skunks average about 10 pounds in weight and may measure as long as 30 inches. All are armed with the same potent spray gun which is accurate up to a dozen feet. However, they usually are harmless if not threatened, and give fair warning when about to "fire" by stamping their feet in anger. They have one litter a year of from one to ten babies. They devour great quantities of mice and insects of all kinds, as well as eggs when they can get them. They enjoy turtle eggs especially. These skunks often visit campgrounds looking for food scraps.

Marten

The marten, also known as sable, resembles a king-sized red squirrel. It is about 2 feet long and weighs about 4 pounds. Martens are lightning fast in the trees and can easily catch a red squirrel. They live on squirrels, birds, mice, eggs, and even larger game when they can catch them. They are a rich brown color with an irregular whitish or yellowish patch on the underside of the throat. Their ears are pointed and also light on the inside. They have one litter a year consisting of from one to five young. Their den is in a hollow tree or is a snug burrow in the ground lined with soft grasses. They live for about 17 years.

Wolverine

The largest of the weasel family, as well as the most elusive and unpleasant, is the wolverine. This animal weighs over 40 pounds and is nearly 4 feet long. He is a clever and vicious animal, destroying anything he finds in the line of food. If he can not eat it himself he will spray it with a vile liquid so that no one else can. He will follow a trapline, killing and tearing to shreds any animal that has been trapped, and he will fight off even a bear or mountain lion, and can kill elk or moose if they are trapped in deep snow. Wolverines are rarely seen in our National Parks except in the wildest and most remote areas, such as in Glacier and McKinley National Parks. Their color is dark brown with a paler yellowish band across rump and up along both sides and a light patch on the chest. Their tails are short and bushy and their ears are rounded and set close to their heads. They can drag a carcass three times their own weight for over a mile across rugged terrain with apparent ease. If they can gnaw and tear their way into a cabin, they will wreck the interior completely and ruin everything in sight with their skunklike spray.

Porcupine

Undoubtedly some of you have seen a slow-moving "porky" or "quill pig" as the porcupine is often called. There are several kinds of porcupines, some small and black and some almost white in color, like this fine specimen from Carlsbad Caverns National Park. In timberland areas outside of a Park they are often killed upon sight, for they do great damage to trees by eating the bark and wood, thus killing the tree. "Porkies" may weigh as much as 40 pounds and are about 30 inches in length. They cannot shoot their barbed quills but can switch their armed tails, driving the barbs into a man or animal. These barbs work their way into the flesh quickly, and must be removed at once with a quick yank, painful as it may be. Porcupines have one offspring, or occasionally twins, in the spring. They are found all over the northern and western parts of the country and about the only animal who kills them successfully for food is the Fisher, another large weasel. Porcupines love salt and will quickly ruin paddles, ax handles, hunting knives and gunstocks smelling of salty perspiration and carelessly left where they can get at them. They move slowly and are the only animal a starving man can kill easily for food with just a club.

Muskrat

Many a country boy has made important pocket money or started his education with funds made by trapping muskrats and selling their pelts to fur dealers. These huge water rats build domed houses from mud, reeds, grass and some small sticks, in swamps and wet lands. They average about 2 feet in length and their tail is slightly flattened on the sides. They weigh about 3 pounds. They provide more fur pelts than all other American mammals combined, and are found in almost every part of our land. They feed on swamp plants, fish and some clams. They raise several litters every year and each litter may have up to ten of the little rodents, so there will always be an abundance for the country boy to pursue. Muskrats can be found along riverbanks and pond shores, even close to big cities, so keep an eye out for these interesting neighbors.

Beaver

The beaver, one of the most important mammals to this continent, has started fortunes, changed the economy and been a legend for centuries. His pelt has been used for currency and was a symbol of wealth, and his image has become the official symbol of some Canadian societies and associations. We admire his energy and the phrase "busy as a beaver" is a very popular expression. He helped start the great Hudson's Bay Company and his engineering feats have been the envy of many a human engineer. This great rodent with the flat and scaly tail measures up to nearly 4 feet in length and may weigh as much as 60 pounds. Typical beaver dams and beaver houses may be found over much of our land and in many National Parks where beavers are tourist attractions. They eat the inner bark of trees and water plants, and store food for the winter. Beavers mate for life and have a litter of two to six offspring every year. They slap the water with their tails as a warning of danger and if one of their dams is damaged, they will repair it overnight. Occasionally they will also build dens in stream or lake banks and dig an underwater entrance to reach them. The beaver is a remarkable and valuable fur bearer and a fascinating animal to watch.

Opossum

The opossum is one of the animals known as a marsupial or "pouched animal." When the young are born they are smaller than a honeybee, yet by pure instinct they can crawl into the fur-lined pouch of the female and attach themselves to the nipples. Out of the fifteen or twenty opossums born at a time, only those able to find a nipple to hang on to survive; the rest die. An adult opossum weighs about 5 pounds and will measure about 3 feet in length. They live on fruit, vegetables, garbage and poultry. They are dirty animals and their dens are usually filthy with refuse. They have two litters a year, and the young travel with their mother hanging onto her fur or tail with their claws and tails. When disturbed, opossums may pretend to be dead ("playing possum"), hide, threaten and then flee, or in rare cases, actually fight. They are found over most of the South and Midwest, and are extending their range into New England. Their coats are gray, white and black and their noses, tails and feet are pinkish. They are good eating and in spite of being hunted continually are increasing in number. They are slow moving and can be caught by hand.

Raccoon

These intelligent and ingenious animals are common over almost all of our country from coast to coast except in desert areas. They are often found living very close to our largest cities. The author lives within sight of New York City yet feeds several raccoons every night at his back door. They are about 30 inches long and may weigh as much as 25 or 30 pounds. They eat almost anything including vegetables, corn, poultry, fish, rodents, frogs, and, contrary to popular belief, do not always wash their food, even when water is provided. If they catch frogs or crawfish, they may swish them in water to remove sand or dirt however. They are generally brownish-gray in color with brown-and-cream striped or banded tails. The black band or "mask" across the eyes is their trademark. They have litters of about one to six young born in the spring and take good care of their offspring. They are vicious fighters when cornered and will try to drown attacking dogs if they are attacked in water. They live in hollow trees, stumps or cement culverts or drainpipes. They make good pets if caught while very young, but are very clever at opening locks, hasps or even untying ropes designed to hold them.

Coatimundi

The coatimundi (above right), a small relative of the well-known raccoon, is often called just "coati." Coatis are found in some of the National Parks in the Southwest, and often travel in small bands. They have long, pointed, turned-up noses, and unlike raccoons they have stripes only on the upper side of the tail, not clear around. They live on insects, worms, birds, mice, fruit, and some plant material. They are long and slender with shorter front legs than hind legs and a tail as long as the body. Their total length is over 50 inches and they weigh up to 25 pounds. They make fine pets but can fight furiously when angered or cornered. There are four to six young in a litter born in early spring. These interesting and inquisitive little mammals are active both day and night but usually around noon and midnight they take it easy or sleep. The face is marked with gray and black, as can be seen in the photo, while the rest of the body color is reddish brown-gray to almost black. The long tail is usually carried straight up in the air with the very tip sharply curled back.

Ringtail

This interesting animal with the fantastic ringed tail is, like the coati, also related to the raccoon. He is also known by the name of civet cat, but ringtail is his most popular name. He is found along our West Coast and in our Southwest. Ringtails are about 3 feet long and weigh about 2 or 3 pounds. They live on small mammals, birds, fruit and sometimes eggs. They hunt mostly at night, spending the daylight hours curled up in their dens in rocks or hollow trees. Their young number from one to five and are born in the spring, covered with a white fuzz and weighing about an ounce apiece. The animal has a brownish-gray back, a lighter underneath, black and white tail bands, a whitish snout and rings around his eyes. A dark spot in front of each eye makes the face unmistakable. Ringtails are preyed upon by larger animals and by the big horned owls that also hunt at night. This animal appears in color on the cover, and also on opposite page (left).

Kit Fox

There are several species of foxes found in our National Parks including the red fox, gray fox, and kit fox. The last, being our smallest, is shown here. These little foxes stand about 1 foot high and measure about 30 inches long. They are gray to pale yellowish-brown in color with a dark almost black spot on either side of the snout and at the tip of the tail. The kit fox so closely matches the arid areas in our Southwest, in which he is found that he is difficult to see, even at close range. He lives on desert rodents, insects, lizards and birds. He is very swift, and after catching his prey usually carries it back to his den, where he can eat it away from danger. The cubs, numbering from four to seven, are born in February or later, even in the spring. This little fox has very large ears and in spite of its intelligent face is not as smart as the familiar red fox. He is very shy and hunts almost entirely at night, spending the rest of the time in underground dens.

Red Fox

Perhaps the one animal most familiar in legend and fairy tale for his intelligence and colorful coat is the red fox. He is a fine reddish-orange color with a darker tail with a white tip, and black feet and legs. His underside is creamy white and his ears are black-tipped. One litter of this handsome animal may include the so-called "silver fox" (all black tipped with silver with a white tail tip), the cross fox (brownish-gray with black feet and legs and a white tail tip) and the black fox (jet black all over except for the white tail tip). All these foxes belong to the same species; merely different color phases. They live on small mammals of all kinds, poultry, and fruit as well as birds. They are found from Alaska across the continent to our Southwest and in almost every National Park. They have a litter of from four to ten cubs in the spring. An adult red fox measures about 42 inches in length and may weigh up to 15 pounds. They are handsome, intelligent and have added much to the color and interest of our countryside for ages past and probably will be around as long as man himself.

Wolf

Another animal very difficult to photograph in the wilds is the timber wolf shown above. These animals are found in several of our National Parks although they are not numerous in any of them. They once roamed all over the North American continent from coast to coast and from the arctic down to Mexico. Now they are mostly found in Canada and a few small areas in the United States where they are protected as National Park residents. They may weigh as much as 150 pounds, stand 30 inches at the shoulder and measure 6 feet in length. They live on anything from mice to moose. A lone wolf can bring down a steer and kill it, and a pack of wolves can tackle anything for food. The author has taped the howls of packs of wild wolves in Canada and there is no wilder music in the world than the howls of a pack of hungry timber wolves out on a night hunting trip! Some wolves are almost reddish in color, others gray and white, some almost black, and the arctic wolves are usually snow-white. They have litters of from three to thirteen pups in the spring and they are well cared for. The pups stay with the parents for a year learning to hunt, and then leave. Wolves live for about fifteen years. Some wolves have been tamed when captured as pups and make good pets.

Coyote

What would a western movie be without the howl of a coyote! These small relatives of the wolf measure about 4 feet long and weigh between 25 and 30 pounds, with the females weighing slightly less than the males, as in most species. Coyotes are grayish-brown on the back and lighter underneath. The tail is tipped with black and the lips and throat are creamy white. Coyotes often hunt in pairs, one driving the quarry toward the other who waits for the kill. They are intelligent animals and do a great deal to keep down the number of rabbits, mice, insects and other rodents of the plain areas. Occasionally they will kill deserted newborn horses, cattle, sheep and goats, but will leave them alone if the parents are nearby. They have five to ten pups in a litter, and live to be about fourteen years old. When running, they usually carry their bushy tail low instead of high as do wolves, their next of kin.

Bobcat

Also known as the wildcat or bay lynx, the bobcat is a smaller version of the big Canada lynx. He is found in many parts of the United States and in most National Parks where there is an abundant supply of small game. The bobcat measures up to between 3 and 4 feet in length and may weigh up to nearly 50 pounds, although the average is about half that. Bobcats live on rabbits, vegetables (if fresh meat is hard to find), birds, rodents of all kinds and some small animals such as calves, fawns, etc. They live in dens in rocks or occasionally a hollow log. In contrast to the Canada lynx, the black on the tip of a bobcat's tail just covers the top, while the entire tip of the lynx's tail is black, and the bobcat's ears are not tufted with long hairs as are those of the lynx — two ways to tell them apart. Both are brownish-gray in color and dappled with darker spots, although the lynx is lighter colored as a general rule. Bobcats are found in deep woods as well as in desert country and swampy areas. The young kittens are born in the spring and number from one to four. Bobcats make a hair-raising screech when startled which in turn will startle almost anyone who hears it.

Mountain Lion

Our only really big cat is the mountain lion, which perhaps has more names than any other single animal in the world. I believe there are nineteen in all, including panther, cougar, puma, painter, catamount, etc. The mountain lion is over 8 feet long and may weigh more than 200 pounds. It is a tawny yellow with a creamy-white underside. It has a small head and a long heavy tail which it uses for balance when making long leaps. It can leap fifteen feet upwards and from a height of sixty feet in safety. Although shy, elusive and almost impossible to see in its native habitat, it can be bold and fearless if required. Mountain lions live on any type of meat, from small rodents up to and including deer, moose and cattle. They usually avoid man but have been known to attack lone children. They can drag a moose weighing over 900 pounds through snow for many yards with apparent ease. They are found in many of our National Parks where their frightening and hair-raising scream, like a woman or child in great pain, is occasionally heard. Mountain lions pair for life and raise from one to five cubs every year. These picturesque and exciting cats should be protected outside our great National Parks as well as inside, for they are diminishing in number.

Black Bear

Although this shaggy resident of much of our country, and in particular in some of our National Parks, is called a "black" bear, he appears in a variety of colors, often several shades appearing in the same litter of cubs. Some are almost blond while others are dark brown and some even have white patches on their chests. The most common of course is all-black with a tan nose. These bears can weigh as much as 500 pounds, although the average is between 2 and 3 hundred pounds. They measure about 6 feet in length, and stand over 3 feet high at the shoulder. They live on small mammals, fish, plants and berries, as well as garbage found around cabins, resorts and campgrounds. In Yellowstone Park they mingle with the campers, raiding garbage pails even while campers watch and take pictures. The young cubs, usually two in number but sometimes as many as four, are born during the winter when the mother is dormant and said to be hibernating. They make their winter dens in caves, hollow logs or under stumps. The author has tracked them many times within comparatively a few miles of New York City. They have a litter only every other year, so should be well protected by short hunting seasons, as in many states, to preserve the species. They can climb trees with great speed and are seldom dangerous to man unless with cubs or if cornered, when they are terrible fighters.

Grizzly Bear

Almost a trademark of the West, the huge grizzly bear is slowly becoming a vanishing species, except in a few National Parks, and one or two Canadian areas extremely remote to hunters. This giant can weigh as much as 1,100 pounds, although the average tips the scales at about 900 pounds. Grizzlies measure nearly 9 feet in length and stand about 4 feet high at the shoulder, or even more. They live on gophers and other rodents, ground squirrels, fish, snakes, grass, fruits and vegetables. They also occasionally kill cattle, goats, hogs, horses and sheep, and will kill deer as well. They are potentially very dangerous to man and should be avoided, especially when they have cubs. They are a tourist attraction in several National Parks, where they come to feed at garbage pits near resorts and campgrounds. There is only one larger bear, the giant Alaskan brown bear or "Kodiak" bear, found in a few areas on islands off the coast of the state of Alaska. These grow to weigh as much as 1,500 pounds and measure 9 feet in length. Grizzly bears have one to four cubs, as do the black bears, weighing a little more than a pound at birth. Fortunately for many hunters, grizzly bears cannot climb trees, although they can outrun a horse for short distances on the ground.

Collared Peccary

These two little members of the "cloven hoof clan" differ from true swine in that they have musk (scent) glands, do not have a small outer hoof on the hind feet and have straight downward-pointing tusks in the upper jaw. Otherwise they look like small pigs. They are also known as musk hogs or javeline (pronounced "hav-a-leen-a") and are found in our Big Bend National Park, in Texas, where over 3,000 roam at will. They stand about 20 inches high, weigh about 65 pounds and measure about 3 feet in length. They live on nuts, grain, vegetables, and fruit. They also eat frogs, snakes, insects, and roots. Their color is blackish-brown with a whitish stripe or "collar" around their shoulders. They have a large scent gland on their backs with which they mark rubbing "posts." They have a litter of from one to two offspring at almost any time of the year, born in a cave or hollow log. A herd of peccaries (some species of these animals run as many as a hundred or more together) is called a "sounder," although the collared peccary is usually seen in pairs or perhaps a small family group. They can be savage and have often treed a hunter for some time.

Pronghorn Antelope

The graceful and speedy pronghorn antelope is truly American for it is found nowhere else, and it is actually not an antelope in the Old World antelope sense. It is more closely related to the sheep. It is the only horned mammal that sheds the outer covering of his horns each year. He stands about 3 feet at the shoulder, and weighs up to 150 pounds. The females are slightly smaller but also have horns. These antelopes usually depend upon their speed for safety as they can run up to fifty miles an hour. They are brownish-tan with white rumps, undersides and two bars across the throat. There are white markings on the face also, and they have a black nose and "chin strap" band below the lower jaw. They have such startlingly white rumps which flash when they run that they are easily spotted. They feed on grass and vegetation and years ago there was an estimated 40 million of these speedy animals on our western plains. They were easily killed as their great curiosity would lure them close to hunters waving a piece of cloth or a hat. Now they are smarter and fewer in number, approximately one or two hundred thousand. They can be seen in many of our National Parks where they are protected of course. They have two or three offspring a year and within ten days the young can outrace a fast dog.

Mountain Goat

These elusive goats are actually more like antelopes than true goats, and are related to the chamois of the Alps. They are short-horned, shaggy animals, and rarely seen, except in Glacier National Park, in Montana, where they have been protected. They live in the highest and most rugged areas of the mountains and feed on anything green they can find there. In the winter they come down to lower levels. They are preyed upon by wolves, bear and even foxes when they are young, but the mothers fight efficiently with their sharp, foot-long horns to protect their kids. They weigh up to 300 pounds, stand about 3 feet high, and measure from 5 to 6 feet in length. Their young number one or two. They are born in late spring and within a half hour can run and jump quite well. These elusive animals with the black horns and white beards can scale almost vertical rock walls and make astonishing leaps without falling. They stay white all year around and travel in small groups, usually all members of the same family.

Mountain Sheep

The mountain sheep, or bighorn sheep as they are often called, are found in over a half dozen of our great National Parks; as many as 3,500 are in Mt. McKinley National Park in Alaska. These magnificent animals with the great curling horns have been hunted as trophies for a century or more but still seem to be doing well in protected areas and the Parks. They weigh as much as 320 pounds, stand over 3 feet at the shoulder and are nearly 7 feet long. The horns of the rams may measure 4 feet along the curve, while those of the females, or ewes, measure less than half this and are straighter. The rams battle furiously for the females in November and the noise of their fighting can be heard for miles. Mountain sheep must have water every day, and salt frequently. They feed on anything green but can get along with a minimum of food. They have one or two lambs in a litter and within two hours they can run and skip about. They have a brownish-gray back and brownish sides, are lighter underneath and have a light colored rump with a dark tail. The end of the nose and chin is also light colored. They usually live in small bands of six or more.

Black-Tailed Deer and White-Tailed Deer

These two examples of America's fine deer are typical of those seen in and around our National Parks. The black-tailed deer above was photographed in the junglelike Olympic National Park, in Washington, while the splendid white-tailed or Virginia deer opposite was photographed in Montana. The black-tailed deer is a western subspecies and its trademark is its black tail. These deer weigh up to 300 pounds, stand 3½ feet high and may be 7 feet in length. The white-tailed deer is about the same size, but may stand a bit higher at the shoulder. The white-tailed deer is found almost all over the country except in the Far West, and even there in small areas. There are more of these deer now than when the Pilgrims landed and they are increasing. The antlers of these two deer vary in shape. Those of the black-tailed deer fork, while those of the white-tailed deer have a main beam with points rising from it. Both live on evergreen browse and hardwood twigs. The white-tailed deer is reddish-brown in summer and grayish in winter. The black-tailed is inclined to be more gray in color. Both have one or two fawns in the spring and the fawns of both species are spotted. Both have scent glands on the inside of the hind legs.

Mule Deer

This alert and handsome example of our fine mule deer was photographed in Grand Canyon National Park, Arizona. These animals are so called because of their huge ears, larger than those of the white-tailed deer. The tail too is more slender than the tail of the black-tailed or white-tailed deer. These fine deer often weigh as much as 400 pounds and are the largest of the three. They are longer than the other two deer, and do not carry their tails high, even when fleeing danger. The white-tailed deer is particularly noted for its white tail held stiffly erect when fleeing an enemy, making it easy for others in the herd to follow. The mule deer also has much larger scent glands on the inside of the hind legs than do the other two species. (The black-tailed is now considered a subspecies rather than a separate species) "Mulies" feed on vegetation, twigs, evergreens and some fruit, as do the other two. Every year they have one to three fawns, also spotted. All deer fall prey to bears, mountain lions, wolves, and, when young, bobcats and lynx. They also occasionally eat themselves out of food and have to be harvested by hunters or moved away to prevent starvation. The antlers of the mule deer fork like those of the black-tailed deer. Female deer or "does" do not have antlers.

Caribou

Although caribou, or reindeer, are only found in one of our National Parks, there are plenty of them in that Park, in fact over 10,000. This great herd of these interesting members of the deer family is found in Mt. McKinley National Park, in Alaska. Here they are protected against all but their natural enemies, which help keep aged, sick and weakly members of the herd at a minimum. Caribou weigh up to 400 pounds and stand 4 feet high at the shoulder. They are about the only member of the deer family in which both males and females have antlers. They live on moss and other types of vegetation local to their areas. The calves are born in the early spring and number one or two. There are several kinds of caribou, the woodlands caribou, found in southern Canada which weigh up to 700 pounds, the barren-ground caribou, a smaller animal found in northern Canada, and the old world caribou introduced into Alaska from Siberia in 1891, a smaller, darker and shorter-legged variety. The real reindeer are domesticated old world caribou. The photo at the right shows caribou (male left, female right) with the "horns" in "velvet" before they are fully developed. Later on, this velvety outer antler covering is rubbed off by the animals against trees and bushes. Domesticated caribou carry heavy loads and pull sleds. They can swim well and travel 100 miles a day.

Elk

One of the most majestic-looking of all the deer is the elk or, as the Indians called it, wapiti. A big elk bull can weigh up to almost 1,000 pounds. Elk stand over 5 feet at the shoulder and are about 9 feet in length. The cows are smaller and unlike the female caribous have no horns. The towering antlers sometimes reach a length of 5 feet from base to tip. The animals are grayish-brown, with a dark thick mane of a chestnut color which extends along over the shoulders where the hair is shorter. The rump is lighter and grayer while the head is dark like the mane. Their young are born in the spring and like other young deer have spotted coats for a few months. The spots then fade and the animal takes on the coloring of its parents. The animals feed on twigs, grass, leaves and small plants high in the mountains in summer, but when the snows come they migrate to lower and warmer areas in the valleys and lowlands. Elk were originally found over most of the United States from New England to California, but now they are restricted almost entirely to a few areas and our National Parks, particularly the vast Jackson Hole Elk Preserve in Wyoming and Yellowstone National Park. Winter feeding by Rangers keeps herds increasing.

Moose

The largest member of the deer family is the moose, sometimes reaching nearly a ton in weight and standing almost 8 feet high at the shoulder. These animals may be 10 feet long and have great "rocking chair" antlers with a spread of 6 feet. They are truly gigantic creatures with forequarters heavier than the hindquarters, an almost nonexistent tail and a heavy "bell" under the throat. They often have a heavy mane, similar to that of the elk. The antlerless cows are smaller. They bear one to three calves in the spring, but unlike most young deer, they are not spotted, but a dark reddish-brown. Moose were originally found all over New England but now they are mostly north of the Canadian border, and in some of our western and midwestern National Parks. They feed on hardwood browse but particularly like the underwater parts of water lilies and other water plants. During the mating season in the fall, bulls are particularly dangerous, and in Canada and Alaska they have even challenged railroad trains in battle. They are homely but heroic animals!

Bison

The largest animal in North America in historic times is the buffalo, or to be correct, the bison, which once roamed the country from the western plains as far east as Pennsylvania. These animals, once numbering countless millions, almost vanished forever at the turn of the century due to slaughter for meat and hides as well as to help starve out the Indians who depended upon them. There were less than 1,000 of them by 1889; some say only 75 were left by 1885. Thanks to desperate conservation measures and government funds they were saved and now there is no danger of extinction. In all it is estimated there are about 25,000 of them in our National Parks and Canadian parks. The Canadian bison are woodland bison, darker and a bit larger, a subspecies of our once great herds. Our buffalo is a dark chocolate-brown with short horns and a tufted tail. They may weigh over 2,200 pounds but average about 1,800 pounds. They stand 6 feet at the shoulder and may be 10 feet long. The cows are smaller but also have horns, as the animal belongs to the cattle family rather than the deer family. Only one calf is born a year but a cow may have one every year for as many as thirty years. Buffalo are grazing animals and roam their ranges in search of food because they crop the grass so short they cannot stay in one place. The saving of these great beasts from extinction was a classic example of what conservation can do when a nation is aroused.